RECOVERY ..... Food For The Soul

STEPS ..... On A Spiritual Journey

Volume 3
INSPIRATIONAL MESSAGES

i

RECOVERY -
Food For The Soul

STEPS .....
On A Spiritual Journey

Volume 3

INSPIRATIONAL MESSAGES

BY

HOPE ULCH BROWN

HUB PUBLISHING

For copies contact:

HUB PUBLISHING

e-mail:
hbrown5667@comcast.net

Phone:
(248) 673-5667

Printed USA by
Harlo Press, 50 Victor, Detroit, Michigan 48203

HUB PUBLISHING

INTRODUCTION

In 1981, my husband of nearly 15 years and I separated and later divorced. I became the single mother of four young children ... ages 5-8-11 and 13 .... and a member of a 12 Step program for families of alcoholics. Thus, MY JOURNEY BEGAN!

This book is a compilation of Christian teachings and values combined with the tools and blueprint of the 12 Step program of recovery .... both of which are SPIRITUAL. Therefore, the title

RECOVERY - Food for the Soul
STEPS ... on a Spiritual Journey
Vol 3

I hope you find these messages as inspirational and beneficial when reading them as they were for me to write.

With love,
    In Christ and the Fellowship,

HOPE

1

DEDICATED ....

TO ..... My parents, children, grandchildren, family and friends.

TO ..... The members of the 12 Step Fellowships and St. Benedict's Choir and Church.

TO ..... All those who have so deeply touched my life on this "road of recovery."

TO ..... St. Therese, The Little Flower, for her guidance, inspiration and all the roses she has sent to me.

TO ..... Our God for all the blessings He has bestowed upon us all.

ALPHABETICAL INDEX

THE 3 A'S

There's **AWARENESS, ACCEPTANCE and ACTION,**
 This progression must become very clear
For where I am, I must be AWARE,
 Of the **ROLE I PLAYED** getting to here.
If I don't like this spot, then I need make a change,
 But first must **ACCEPT** what has happened.
The past it is over and can't be brought back,
 But my spirits they don't have to dampen.
So I ACCEPT the things I cannot change,
 Like....all others, and what's already done,
Take action so not to repeat it again,
 For the past, it is what I LEARN from.
So, **FIRST I'm AWARE .... then ACCEPT** what is done,
 And take **ACTION** for better positions,
If I follow this process, day after day,
 It's not hard to make needed transitions.

AM I A VICTIM?

Am I really a "victim" today?
Do I just lie down on the ground?
Letting others walk all over me?
How ridiculous does that sound?

And when I'm in that **"victim role,"**
It's soon I start to resent,
All the things that are happening,
And the pain it doesn't relent.

Being a **"victim"**.... that choice is mine,
There's no one can make me submit,
It's something that I have **"volunteered"** for,
And up to me, to make myself quit!

The only way to get rid of pain,
Is **EMPOWER** myself and stand up,
And say that that's all I am going to take,
And begin to fill **MY OWN** cup.

I must become .... important ... have worth,
Do for me what I need to do,
RESPECT MYSELF and **TRUST MY GOD.**
And let you take care of you!

AT HIS TABLE

It was at the table of the Lord,
   That the bread and wine were given,
He came to sacrifice his life,
   Conquer death ... angels said, "He's risen."
It shows the ultimate **LOVE** of God,
   HIS SON came to set us free,
We sit at that same table today,
   He said, "Do in remembrance of me."
When we receive His body and blood,
   Out of love we're forever grateful,
For the ultimate sacrifice He made,
   And the **GRACE** we receive **AT HIS TABLE**.

AN APOSTLE NAMED THERESE

I had a friend ... her name was Therese,
  She was like a Grandmother to me,
    She truly exemplified the words,
      "I was blind ... but now I see,"
She lived for over 100 years,
  Just imagine the experiences she had,
    Some times of joy and wonderment,
      Some very, very, sad.
She was the most "devoted" being,
  Because her life reflected **HIM,**
    Her journey was with Jesus Christ,
      Even when her sight, it dimmed.
Where she lived, she called HIS HOUSE,
  Because Jesus dwelt within,
    Yes, it was their dwelling place,
      Away from the world and sin.
In 1949, life changed,
  She found **sobriety**,
    She shared her wisdom, love of God,
      That finally set her **"free."**
She met with Bill and Dr. Bob,
  Who were inspired by the Lord,
    To formulate 12-Steps for life,
      Which she followed in accord.
She was by all accounts in life,
  The most **"spiritual"** person I've known,
    A true "apostle" of the Lord,
      And with Him was never alone.

She taught me oh, so many things,
  Always said that **"God is LOVE."**
    And surrounded herself with angels who,
    Watched over her from above.
She said, "Don't ever let your mind,
  Wander way out ... on a trip,
    It's too little to be out all by itself,
    Take God along, or you will slip."
She taught me that Bill W. said,
  In order to stop the drinking,
    We can't make changes in ourselves,
    Unless, we change our **THINKING**.
With her quiet ways and gentleness,
  She spread "the word" on many missions,
    But you better know her feistiness,
    If you omitted "steps" and "traditions."
With her list of physical maladies,
  She smiled and never complained,
    Lit up while saying, "Oh, God is so good,
    With all these ailments....I have no pain!"
She had a wonderful walk with God,
  Often spoke of the "Mt. Top High,"
    Her desire to be united with HIM,
    Come October 23, two-thousand and five.
I'm sure HE smiled upon her face,
  And said "Welcome dear servant, well done!
    You've earned a well deserved rest,
    With Our Father, we're glad you've come!"

Dedicated to Therese S. 1905-2005 One of the "Kings' Kids"
Sobriety Date November 30,1949

ATTITUDE

We don't always get from life,
Our every whim and desire,
Often with our traumas and trials,
We find it's hard not to tire,

Yet, there are those, who see the rain,
And feel depressed by the hour,
While others see the same drops fall,
And say IT WILL HELP THE FLOWER.

It's our ATTITUDE that dictates,
Just how well we cope,
If it's very optimistic,
Then there is always hope.

So ACCEPT the things you cannot change,
CHANGE to positives, things you CONTROL,
This is a fact....by which we should act,
Then with life's punches we can roll!

BEGINNING TO END

Life it really isn't hard,
Even through trials and pain,
Because I need just call on HIM,
And invoke His **HOLY NAME**.

"Sweet Jesus", I ask, "Watch over me,
Guide me each step of the way,
Enlighten me to do **YOUR WILL**"
Is what I need to pray.

Accept the things I cannot change,
Change what I can, not live in **FEAR,**
Be honest with others, and true to myself,
And make sure **HIS WORDS** I hear.

I cannot always see the way,
My heavenly Father is my guide,
I need not worry, be discontent,
If I'm walking by **HIS SIDE.**

He's given me the Eucharist,
Providing graces that I need,
So that I might live my life,
In peace....in word and deed.

"Thank you Lord for being there,
You're my solace, joy...my friend,
For you're the ONLY one I have,
Who's with me....**BEGINNING TO END!"**

CHOICES

Our lives are filled with choices,
About families, jobs and friends.
From the time we get up 'til we go to bed,
To them, there is no end.

Do we want to laugh or cry,
Sometimes smile or frown?
Do we solve problems easily,
Or find we often compound?

First, we must understand ourselves,
Just what is it we can do?
Take a look at the options,
But first **to ourselves be true.**

We must make choices acceptable,
For us it must be the right action,
We know when they are comfortable,
'cause with them comes self -satisfaction.

Sometimes with problems, we're too involved
And can't see the trees for the forest.
If we don't look at them objectively,
Our **EMOTIONS** can destroy us.

There is no one else we **CONTROL,**
Yet, others are part of our lives.
How much they inf luence what we do,
Is up to us to **DECIDE**

The **CHOICES** we make in the future,
Will be better than days gone by,
Because after failures, we have learned
And have experience on our side.

We'll forever be faced with decisions,
And there's only us to blame,
If life is not going the way we like,
Then it's our **CHOICES** we'll have to **CHANGE**

CHRISTMAS HIS JOURNEY BEGAN

"**GIVE GLORY TO GOD**" the angels sang,
  on that glorious Christmas morn,
    a stable, a babe in the manger lay,
      the Son of God, my Savior, was born.
'Twas Mary and Joseph and animals 'round,
  to give praise this wondrous birth,
    and wise men three, with incense, gold and myrrh,
    who traveled half way across earth.
They followed the star to Bethlehem,
  that foretold of this greatest event,
    they found in their presence the King of Kings,
    as the prophets foretold, He was sent.
And an angel appeared so that Joseph would know,
  that Jesus would be the child's name,
    His mission on earth to redeem us all,
    "Our Savior" the world would proclaim.
In His life He'd perform many miracles,
  as human, feel joy, suffering, pain,
    and after His death to redeem us all,
    He would someday return again.
Yes, it all began on that Christmas morn,
  the journey that my Savior trod,
    the one who **LOVES** me most of all,
    My brother....my friend....Son of God.

CHRISTMAS JOY ALL YEAR

Christmas is the time of year,
For hearing sleigh bells ring,
The coming of our Christ and Lord,
We hear the angels sing.

For it is, the star on high,
That shines its wondrous light,
The new born babe in Bethlehem,
Beheld by shepherd's sight.

Throughout the centuries we've prayed,
On this same Christmas day,
For God to bless our families,
And guide us in our ways.

The journey we each come to know,
Each day we live our life,
Is done in glory for our **KING,**
Who guides us through life's strife.

This season came to us that day,
He bore our sins and fears,
So we can celebrate **HIS LIFE,**
The Christmas JOY....**ALL YEAR!**

MORE THOUGHTS ......

CHRIST SAID....

You are to "love one another,"
in the same way that "I have loved you."
This isn't simply done through **WORDS,**
but shown in the things that you **DO!**

THE STONE

"Let those who are without sin,
    be the first to cast a stone."
    And if we all were **HONEST**
    there's not one that would be thrown.

YOU'LL BE SAFE

The past it is over....the future's not here
It's today I'll enjoy;
        The Lord said "Have no fear."
I'll take care of your lives,
    There'll be joy and some weeping,
        So take my hand children,
            You'll be safe in my keeping.

A FEW MORE THOUGHTS ......

When I'm looking out for you,
  Instead of taking care of me,
    That is what is better known,
      As **CODEPENDENCY!**

LESSON LEARNED

The more and more I grow,
  The more and more I know,
    My most important lesson learned,
      Is **ASK GOD'S HELP** and then **LET GO!**

PERCEPTION

Dear God I need to walk with you,
  So I can get a different view.

ERROR

Sin starts out as an **ERROR** in thought,
  That we have a chance to correct,
    We ask God for His will for us,
      And from **ERRORS,** to guide and protect.

CODEPENDENTS .. "I'M SORRY"

Codependents always apologize,
    when they're **not even wrong**,
They're always saying "I'm sorry,"
    It's like the lyrics in a song,
They do this out of habit,
    The objective..."keep the peace,"
For their **self-worth**, is missing,
    Or this behavior, they would cease.
We only need apologize,
    When what we've done is wrong,
It's only in recovery...that...
    We learn to **change** our song.

BALANCE

There's **three** important tasks in life,
    Prayer, recreation and **work,**
When we have **BALANCE** in these things,
    None are obsession....nor are shirked.
To our God, we **pray and meditate,**
    Be still and hear of HIS words,
We **eat** and **sleep** and **play** and **rest,**
    Walk amongst the trees and the birds,
We **work** to use the talents God gave,
    As a source to take care of our needs,
We must have all **three, BALANCED** in us,
    In order that we may succeed.

COINCIDENCES?

There's no such thing as "coincidences."
   It's for us that they were meant,
We couldn't orchestrate them all,
   Therefore, they are **God-sent**.
It simply isn't in our power,
   To make these things take place,
Some things are given us with love,
   Some others are erased.
The **timing** and togetherness,
   Fits like the puzzle parts,
Each piece is in the Master's hand,
   They're given from the heart.
Yes, life is little miracles,
   God-incidences keep us going,
In them we see concern for us,
   For His love is ever showing.

BELIEVING

Seeing is NOT believing,
It's by **BELIEVING** that we **see**,
For our God is all-knowing,
And makes it **CLEAR** to those who **BELIEVE**.

WORDS OF WISDOM

There's something my Dad told me long ago,
  He said, "Honey, life's simple, you see,
    When you're **happy** you **laugh**....when you're **sad** you **cry,**
    Say when you're **angry**....how hard can that be?"

DEALING WITH EMOTIONS

Did you ever notice it's difficult,
To deal with feelings, when they occur?
We stew and mull them over within,
Build them up...'til we're in a furor,
We then make a choice to bury them,
And get knotted up all inside,
Because we lack healthy coping skills,
We just keep them in....we hide.
The other extreme, is to just lash out,
Attack others, and spew our frustration,
Because we're upset, and don't have control,
From feelings, we seek emancipation.
But neither of these, behaviors are healthy,
Avoidance or outright aggression,
What we need to be.....is **ASSERTIVE** enough,
and of our faculties...we keep possession.
We **say** what we **feel**, and ask for our **needs,**
And do it with **calm** and **composure,**
So we don't have to hide, or act out anymore,
And our feelings,...we give them exposure

DECISION

When I make a **God-centered DECISION,**
   About what is right for **ME,**
I need to consider nothing else,
   For others gain also, you see.
For if I'm okay with what I do,
   And my actions bring **ME** peace,
Others will also benefit from this,
   And inner turmoil, it does cease.

POSITIVE POWER

Where there is a will....there is a way,
   It's the **THINKING POSITIVE POWER,**
For us to take action....accomplish good things,
   And on us, God's blessings will shower.

THE KEYS

The **FATHER**....is **KING**
   The **SON**....is the **LORD**
     The **SPIRIT**...the one imparts **WISDOM**.

And so if we have all **THREE** in our lives,
We carry **THE KEYS** to the kingdom.

DELIVERED FROM BONDAGE

The **12-STEPS** were gifts...that were heaven sent,
  Given two men, Bill and Bob,
For they came out of the Bible, you see,
  We're inspirationally sent by God,
Books by James and Paul... Sermon on the Mt.
  Had been truly, divinely inspired.
To deliver these men from their bondage and pain,
  So, together they learned and conspired,
How to tell others, how they were delivered,
  That **"spirituality"** was the only way,
To live a life, in the spirit of God,
  And therefore, to meditate and pray,
But along with prayer, must come the **"works,"**
  Get rid of the negative thoughts,
Be kind to others, and tell the truth,
  It brings serenity that can't be bought!
Not regret the past, just learn from it,
  Not be angry, willful...self-centered,
And delivered from bondage and into the "light,"
  With a Higher Power, a life they re-entered.
Changing their **THINKING** and making **AMENDS**,
  This essential **ACTION** was prime.
Forgiving the past and not looking ahead,
  Living just one day at a time.
The **12- STEPS** .... a **BLUEPRINT**...for living their lives,
  Could only be given by God,
So they could find freedom and happiness,
  As, on this journey, **WITH HIM**, they trod.

DON'T LEAVE

When we go to meetings and tell our story,
It's first about suffering and pain,
We want to know....how to "fix" someone else,
For that is the reason we came.

And then early on, we find it is us,
Who needs to make **CHANGE** in our lives,
For if we don't, the hurt will remain,
And all we will do is survive.

For codependency.... a recovery program,
If we keep coming back we will grow,
We are "our" flower, in the garden of life,
Cast on life's river....we learn how to flow.

The knowledge and wisdom that's shared among all,
The strength to trust God and keep going,
We learn at the tables, with things that are said,
God's in our midst, and He is all-knowing.

We **KEEP COMING BACK,** for His message is here,
And we're taught a new way to live,
Because if we leave, we're no better than thieves,
For we've **TAKEN** and then didn't **GIVE**.

We need to **GIVE** back, in order to keep it,
That's what the twelfth step says to do,
So, even if we.....feel better ourselves,
We **DON"T LEAVE** .... so that others can, too!!!

EXPERIENCE.....THE TEACHER

If we were to live our life over again,
    Would we do the same things the same way?
The answer is "yes", of course we would,
    Our decisions were based on **THAT DAY**.

Whatever we knew, or did not know,
    That's just who we were at the time,
The wisdom has come, through trial and error,
    Through this process, life gets more sublime.

It's not 'til the later years of our life....
    We take stock of mistakes that we've made,
Through trials and struggles and the results,
    That our character flaws seems to fade.

"Experiences are the best teachers", we have,
    And we all have had plenty of those,
It's only by learning from choices we've made,
    That a **NEW LIFE** we learn to compose.

So, if we went back and did it again,
    TODAY....we would differently do it,
But we had to have the **EXPERIENCES** of life,
    And at the time....we hadn't gone through it!

FOLLOW THROUGH

Codependents listen to the words,
  They believe what the addict tells them,
They are in denial of the disease....
  To believe the promises that they sell them.
The addict uses the way he does,
  With both physical and emotional need
For when he tries to give it up,
  His body will crave that he feed.
It's not about what codependents SAY
  Addicts "listen" to what they DO.
And if codependents state a position,
  They NEED to **FOLLOW THROUGH**.
For if they don't... the addict knows,
  That he can get his way,
That's when the addiction, it progresses,
  'Cause codependents don't DO what they SAY.
For it's not 'til the props are pulled from them,
  That the addict can feel his own PAIN
That he has a need for **recovery**,
  And may be able to get SOBER again.

FOOD FOR OUR SOUL

If we're looking to find ... PEACE, LOVE, and JOY,
We must DO the things that Our Lord said,
For at the Last Supper He gave us the words,
As He raised up the wine and the bread,

He said, "This is my body, This is my blood
DO THIS in remembrance of me,"
He gave this to us... as the **"food for our soul,"**
With it graces that we would receive.

It's through the Eucharist, the **"food for our soul,"**
We get strength, for it came from on high
What a wonderful gift, He's given to us,
So be grateful ... AND DON'T PASS IT BY.

GENTLE

We need to be **GENTLE** with ourselves,
For critical ... causes **PAIN**,
ACCEPT our imperfections and...
CHANGE what we can change.

HIS DESIGN

If we pray and meditate with intent,
His **DIRECTIONS**, He will tell,
By going against this Higher Power within,
It takes us straight to h-1.
For it's our choice to follow or not,
And our decisions need align,
So HE ... my heart ... and soul agree,
And my actions match **HIS DESIGN**.

TWO

OVERCOME......with the energy of God's power,
"WE" can do what I can't do,
I know I'm not on this journey alone
When there's God and me.....that's **TWO**

GOD'S GRACE......THE POWER

What is the meaning of **GOD'S GRACE** in our life?
It's the **POWER** that comes from on high,
To right the wrongs that we've done time again,
And to kiss the sick past...good-bye!
We've all made mistakes, done things we're not proud of,
Hurt others and hurt ourselves, too,
God knew we we're human and that we would sin.
So, He sent us HIS SON to undo.
His **GRACE** is the very **STRENGTH** that we need,
To forgive and to change life around,
Let go of addictions and sick behaviors,
So peace and contentment be found.
Get rid of our anger... be calm and patient,
And act with compassion and care,
To go with the flow, and live day by day,
And ask for **GOD'S GRACE** in our prayer.
For it is the **POWER** to make needed changes,
And be humble, lose resentments, have peace.
Ask God for direction and the **STRENGTH** to live,
HIS WILL....then the turmoil does cease.
For **GOD'S GRACE** is given to those who just **ASK**,
At Last Supper said "do this" for me'
He gave us a **means** to acquire **GOD'S GRACE,**
That we needed so we could be **FREE.**
For we are not here, just out on our own,
Jesus cried out for us when He died,
For He bore our sins, and gave freedom to us,
When "Father forgive them," He cried.
GOD'S GRACE is the gift that He gave us all,
It's the **POWER** to overcome sin,
And all the wrongdoings we've done in our life,
To rest with **HIM**, with **PEACE** from within.

GOD'S PLANNED DAY

God teaches me patience in so many ways,
   This test usually comes, when He alters my days,
The plan that I had so carefully crafted.
   As the day goes along, by my God are redrafted.
I think I'll see someone or go here or there,
   And when the day ends, I'll be off...out somewhere,
I never expected, doing things ... going places,
   That were not on my list, and with different faces.
It's God's sense of humor, He just plays with me,
   To see if I'm flexible, accepting and free.
It's my test for FAITH, that God covers my needs,
   I just do my part keeping track of my deeds.
I smile at these tests that God sends my way,
   And pray as I go.....to enjoy **GOD'S PLANNED DAY!**

GOD'S WORLD

When I awake in the morning,
  To the gentle chirping of birds,
    I refer to them as **"GOD'S CHOIR,"**
    No prettier sounds to be heard.

I see nature alive and bustling,
  Squirrels and chipmunks scurry around,
    I feel the sun... breeze through the trees,
    God speaks with these sights and sounds.

I sit here in still contemplation....touched,
  And marvel at what HE has sent,
    In me, HIS wondrous love, JOY abounds,
IN GOD'S WORLD, I find **PEACE...CONTENTMENT.**

INSANITY

To do the same things over and over again,
  And expect to have different outcomes,
There's something wrong with **my THINKING,**
  It's called **"INSANITY"**...it can't be done.
If I always do what I've always done,
  I'll always get what I always got,
So, if I don't like the result that come,
  I have to change **my THINKING,** a lot!!!

Good Orderly Direction

God made us all in His image and likeness,
Knew as humans we'd err and we'd fall,
With a Father's love, He sent us His son,
To die and redeem us all.

He gave **commandments,** (12 steps) **Bible** (Big Book) **Eucharist,**
In order to have His protection,
For us they are.... a BLUEPRINT... for living,
So our lives have **good orderly direction.**

If we pass them by, **these tools** that He gave,
And our lives just go all awry,
There's not much else He can do for us,
For we ignored Him and didn't even try.

Yes, we must be born again, pick up these tools,
Which He gave so we'd turn life around,
We read, we pray, we receive the Eucharist,
Then with freedom and JOY, we abound.

GRATITUDE

I have so much to be **GRATEFUL** for,
The many blessings God has sent,
Even the things He's taken away,
What he left, for me, were meant.

I have a home and nice family,
Food, clothes, good health and more,
Education, transportation, a job, as well,
And my FAITH ....to 'knock" on His door.

He's always there to answer me,
When, with Him, I need to speak,
"My child" he says, "what do you want?"
With my answer, I am meek.

"Dear Lord, I love you very much,
Protect me, my family and all,
Please keep me healthy and close to you,
So, on my journey, I will not fall.

Sometimes, I trip with the choices I make,
But I know you'll help me recover,
Because you're my friend, my guide and support,
And I LOVE YOU as no other!"

HAVE NO DOUBT

Have no doubt about it....in GOD'S WORLD there's
  NO MISTAKES.
It's the human, frail condition, where there's
  errors we do make.
In His Sermon on the Mountain, He said words,
  spelled out the PLAN.
He knew we'd need DIRECTIONS, for we
  are only "man."
There's a blueprint made for living,
  a Book, 12 Steps, His grace.
If we want to find contentment and the pains
  of earth erase.
We must ACCEPT our human weakness....turn will over
  to His care,
And meet each day with peace and joy, even though
  LIFE ISN'T FAIR.
We have to stay in HIS WORLD, not sidetracked by
  things of man,
By walking with each other....for I can't do the
  things WE can.

GRAMMA AND ME

Looking back at my life, when I felt safe and free,
We're the days that I spent, my Grandmother and me,
We'd roll out of bed and then kneel down to pray,
To ask God for blessings and a wonderful day,
I'd watch some TV and then take a shower,
While Gramma cooked breakfast, at some early hour.
We'd feed all the birds and go for a walk
And play silly games, it was just fun to talk.
She said she felt bad for the kids of today,
For it seemed no one listened to what we had to say.
So I'd talk and she'd listen, we'd share thoughts and beliefs,
From our greatest concerns, we'd find some relief.
We'd always play games, dominoes was just one,
We'd laugh and just giggle, having wonderful fun.
Christmas especially, was a great time for me,
We'd drink our hot chocolate and decorate the tree.
If sometimes I'd act like an "imp" she would say,
"Maybe you could do it some other way."
She's not yell or scream, was just matter a fact,
And just simply told me...a new way to act.

We'd laugh as she put the dominoes in the frig,
Or I'd want some lipstick and she'd say "just a smidge."
We'd go to the show, most times we're together,
Get popcorn and slushes, no matter the weather.
At night after dinner, I'd get in the tub,
The jets making bubbles, the soap I would rub.
She'd gather me out, a big towel wrapped around,
And dry off my hair...oh, boy I slept sound.
She'd circle her arms and give a BIG HUG,
And I felt as "snug as a bug in a rug."
But before we'd drift off, many stories we'd read,
Yes, this was the time, I was happy indeed!
We'd again say our prayers, thanking God for our day,
Listing all others, for whom we would pray.
'Twas on Sunday morning, we'd rise and we'd shine,
So we'd get to church and we'd be on time.
For Gramma, she sang in the choir whole hearted.
I'd practice with them before church even started.
We'd warm up our voices and sing out a song,
It was wonderful having a place to belong.
When time spent together was over and done,
I was sad to leave....but I had such great fun!!!

HE'S THE POWER

Isn't it amazing,
Jesus catered to the lame,
The sick and the downtrodden
To Him, is where they came.
For He knew our human weakness,
And the one's He loved most dear,
Were not the powerful and strong,
But those **weak**, who had some **fear**.
For then He could **restore** them,
Those lambs that had been lost,
We know how much He loved us,
For His life, He paid the cost.
It's the souls who are addicted,
And the one's who suffer pain,
That He finds the most loveable,
And the reason that He come.
For HE'S their only **POWER**,
Who restores them to the light,
And when they "knock" upon His door.
It brings Him such **delight**.

HIS CHILDREN

We're each God's representatives,
  This job begins at birth,
For we are all HIS children,
  And reflect **"OUR DAD"** on earth,
So we make sure our actions,
  Are something He'd be proud,
HIS MESSAGE we spread to others,
  Saying "love one another" that's how.
And through the good, bad and ugly
  We teach all to **TRUST HIS POWER.**
For it is ever with us,
  Every minute, day and hour.
Yes, we're each one of the **KING'S KIDS,**
  We're happy to bear His name,
And when He sent His son, Jesus,
  Christians we became.
He gave us the gospels, the **"GOOD NEWS"**
  Of how to get back to our God,
When once we leave this earthly home,
  And this journey on which we have trod.
For He has prepared "many mansions"
  There's one for each and all,
As long as we follow God's blueprint,
  away from evil, so we do not fall.
Yes, we represent OUR FATHER,
  It's up to us to reflect His will,
We live our life, and do our best,
  And for His message, we learn to be **STILL.**

HIS GIFTS

May the **PEACE** of God be with us,

May we **TRUST** He'll "light" our way,

May the **FAITH** of possibilities,

Give us **HOPE** for every day.

May the **LOVE** of God surround us,

May the **SPIRIT** give us lifts,

From **FREEDOM** from life's bondages,

From **OUR FATHER** these are our gifts.

THE LORD SPEAKS

It's in the gentle **stillness,**
That the Lord speaks to our heart,
If we take Him on our journey
Then **WE** never are apart.

HIS MERCIFUL LOVE

My Higher Power... is a God of JUSTICE
    But, of Him, I shall have no fear,
For He wants nothing more for me,
    Than His love, and to draw me near.

Even, for me, when His **JUSTICE** reigns,
    He is **MERCIFUL** when giving His sentence,
For He knows, I have human weakness,
    And for it, I will have some repentance,

But for Him I am not ....a lost little lamb,
    For His **MERCY**, it always seeks me,
So even in **JUSTICE**, my **MERCIFUL** God,
    Wants only for me to be **FREE**.

Not locked in a prison, of my own will and glory,
    But to follow His Word and His Path,
He takes and He shelters me tight in His arms,
    In His MERCY, for me has no wrath,

If I'm trying my best with the struggles in life,
    And make some mistakes in the day,
'tho He is all **JUST**, **HIS MERCIFUL LOVE**,
    Let's me know He's the Truth, Life and Way.

Although He is **JUST**, He is also **FORGIVING**,
    And that's where HIS **MERCY** shines through,
I have to recognize where I am weak,
    And change what I say and I DO.

HIS TEACHINGS

My Christmas this year,
   Is of Sim-pli-city,
I'm just staying home,
   And in His company.

I'm watching the story
   Of Jesus Christ's teaching,
It's really so simple,
   The words of His preaching.

A camel through a needle,
   Is easier to do, .
Than the rich get to heaven,
   'cause they share with so few.

He fed all the throng,
   With the loaves and the fishes
And promised His **PEACE**
   If we'd follow His wishes.

God made Sabbath for man,
   Not the man for the Sabbath,
We need time to be thankful,
   For all that we haveth.

The BLUEPRINT to follow,
   In our life, how to live
In His Sermon on the Mountain,
   Is where He did give.

He forgave Mary Magdelan,
  For all of her sins,
Will He do less for me,
  If I ask from within?

He said sins are forgiven,
  Just do them no more,
And whatever you need,
  Simply 'knock" on His door.

He rose from the dead,
  The sick....healed the lame,
And helped the 'blind see,"
  And for us, does the same.

For **BELIEVING** is seeing,
  When we follow His word,
We see **MIRACLES** all around,
  When His wisdom is heard.

He said the "Qur Father,"
  For that's how to pray,
And He told us that He,
  Is the **TRUTH, LIFE** and **WAY**.

'tho His kingdom's of heaven,
  And not of this earth,
It's with JOY that I celebrate,
  This day of His birth.

HOLIDAY FRENZY

As winter approaches and holidays draw near,
It's supposed to be, a time of good cheer.
Looking forward to Christmas with a child's delight,
And ol' St. Nick down the chimney that night.
We plan for the shopping and hope not to freeze,
Just make it simple, and do it with ease.
Yet, it seems something happens, while executing this plan,
It doesn't turn out......the way it began!

We zip in and out of the stores in a frenzy,
Looking for sales that entice,
A time that's supposed to be full of good cheer,
There's some people who aren't even nice!
Today, with computers, shopping's supposed to be easy,
If you know how to push the right keys,
Order this, order that...go in rooms and just chat,
This year, it will be just a breeze.
But it seems that with all of our best intentions,
There's some things that just go awry,
No matter the planning, we're not in control,
......of others.....oh, don't even try!

There's relatives, of course, who are in a dither,
About whose going where, at what time?
And families descend, and out of town friends,
Pretty soon there's no reason or rhyme.
There's the wrapping of gifts and the tying of bows,
And be sure that you have the tape handy,
And, oh don't forget, to send out of town cards,
And to pick up the holiday candy.
Take the kids places and see Santa Claus,
And stock up on food, dessert, drinks,
Go out to parties, concerts attend,
Our head gets so cluttered, can't think.
The Christmas tree has to be trimmed and lit up,
The outside, it must be decorated.
The cakes and cookies are rolled, sprinkled, baked,
And the jello must be 'frigerated.

Oh......this wonderful time of the year,
If only we don't lose our cool,
Be nice and smile and have a good time,
Let the **ATTITUDE** of **GRATITUDE** rule.!

HOW DOES IT WORK?

What is it about my recovery I'd say?
I know it all starts when I kneel and I pray.
I roll out of bed and get down on my knees,
And ask the Lord's blessing, watch over me please.
For mental and physical and spiritual health,
To know that success is not pride, greed or wealth.
From the bondage of self, I ask for relief,
To do His will and increase my belief.
To just try to be the best person I can,
And with God and the fellowship, walk hand in hand.
For He gave me some books, and great slogans galore,
So that I can improve, my life even more.
I go to my meetings to learn...that is why,
From others, I see, how the steps do apply.
I look at my defects and make my amends,
For any wrongdoing to those I offend.
I have sponsors to talk to, when upset or blue,
Those are the people who help me get through.
I also have strengths that I want to admit,
Knowing what to hang on to....and then what to quit.
At night when my tasks are completed and done,
I again kneel down to thank Father and Son,
And the Holy Spirit for giving me grace,
For these gifts from God, I could never replace.

I BELIEVE

I BELIEVE .... that the morning sun will rise,
I BELIEVE .... that God made the stars, moon and skies,
I BELIEVE .... when we die, Our Savior we'll meet,
I BELIEVE .... my mistakes, I don't have to repeat,
I BELIEVE .... that our God wants to dwell in our hearts, and
stay close to us, so we're never apart.
I BELIEVE .... that God's Son, bore all of our sins,
so heaven's gates opened and we could walk in.
I BELIEVE .... that God loves us most of all,
and for His help...we just need to call.
I BELIEVE .... that the answers God will give to me,
For He is all-knowing, sees the things we don't
see.
I BELIEVE .... that our God will not let us down,
for He's here for us and is always around.
I BELIEVE .... when life's over and with earth we are done,
we'll see the FATHER, HOLY SPIRIT and SON.

I BELIEVE .... man's created for God's honor and glory,
There's a mansion somewhere.....but that's.....the NEXT STORY!

IN HIS HANDS

When I'm plugged in to someone else,
   I go "up and down" with their doing,
I have resentments, hurt and pain,
   And I find that I'm usually "stewing."
About how they need to change their life,
   Act different in their behavior,
But that's self-centered on my part,
   After all, I'm not their savior,
Only He knows.... what's good for them,
   So, **IN HIS HANDS** I place all others,
For I just need to live **MY LIFE**,
   And take my focus off another.

WISE MAN.....FOOL?

Who is a **WISE MAN**......and **WHO IS A FOOL?**
   How is it that we decide?
A **WISE MAN** makes use of the gifts that God sends,
   and it **FOOLS** who just pass them by.
Some of the gifts that God sends to us,
   Are the tools of recovery .... they're free,
The 12-Steps, the books, the meetings and friends,
   so, I'll use them and a **WISE MAN** I'll be!!!

IN THE STILLNESS

Just as we love...each and all of our children,
  Our FATHER, He loves us too,
    It's just their behavior sometimes we don't like,
      Nor OUR FATHER, some things that WE DO.

We must turn our lives, over to HIS CARE.
  And for HIS message...**LISTEN**... **BE STILL**,
    For in the **QUIET**.... we can **HEAR** HIS VOICE,
      And know for us, what is HIS WILL.

United with HIM, and SURRENDERING ourselves,
  Is the way we receive all HIS LOVE,
    'cause when we're busy pursuing our wants,
      We can't receive the messages from above.

When we do OUR WILL, we LIMIT ourselves,
  God wants so much more for us all,
    By thinking we have the best plan for our lives,
      Is when we will tumble and fall.

It is in the **STILLNESS**... we pray... meditate,
  And **LISTEN** for His PLAN...DIRECTIONS,
    For the things, HE wants us to DO in our lives,
      For, with Him, we have a connection.

For the Dear Lord wants nothing more for us all,
  Than be Happy...Joyous...and Free,
    That's why we ask for relief from SELF,
      As we pray, each day, on bended knee.

I RELEASE

I know I can't erase your pain,
   For years, that's what I tried to do,
I've apologized for any pain that I caused,
   In whatever happened to you.

It appears you've a problem, forgiving me,
   Yet, I don't deserve angry outbursts,
Whatever resentment you have inside,
   Is not better, it only gets worse.

Now it's up to you... to heal your past,
   It's not mine, so I can't do it,
Maybe the anger would disappear,
   If you'd forgive, and work your way through it.

There is a wish I have for us,
   That one day we'd relate...just like friends,
For now I reach out... and you just reject me,
   So, it's up to you.... how this story ends.

I care, I love you....that says it all,
   And I wish you joy, happiness, peace,
I'm also seeking the same for myself,
   So in God's hands, I place you.....**I RELEASE!!!**

IT WAS I WHO CARRIED YOU

"For it was I who carried you", the Dear Lord said,
   Through loss and sorrow, anxious moments,
And through times of fear and dread,
   It was I who carried you and held your hand so tight,
In the morning, through the day, into your bed at night.

For I left footprints in the sand and carried you,
   You needed love, I picked you up,
You are my child that's what I do,
   I am shelter from the storm, my arms held and kept you
warm, 'til you had faith to walk the walk and my will to perform.

My dearest child you know that I am your best friend,
   And I will be with you forever, from beginning to the end,
So rest your pain in me and never be afraid,
   For when you falter I am there for comfort and for aid.

......"For it was I who carried you" .... the Dear Lord said.

JOY

Happiness...is not... a destination,
  A place where I arrive,
    It is a way of traveling,
      And the choices I decide.

If I make healthy choices,
  Then happiness appears,
    If life is lacking touch with God,
      Then comes anger, resentment and fears.

Happiness is about my circumstances,
  The surrounding that I choose,
    My friends, my job, my entertainment,
      If unhappy, it's I who'll lose.

JOY is something else, I've learned,
  It's not about my surroundings or others,
    It's about my **relationship** with my **God,**
      Walking hand in hand, I discover.

Just who I am and what I might do,
  To be the person God wants me to be,
    I can have JOY and not happiness,
      Because with God, my life's "spirit-filled"...free!

There's physical pains and disappointments,
  It's hard to be happy through these,
    But I can still...be at peace and JOY filled,
      Because my God He goes through it with me.

JUST WHO AM I?

Just "Who Am I" really?
Why do I act and feel this way?
I'm a product of my environment,
I guess it's safe to say.

The old events that shaped my life,
Have both been good and bad,
Some made me very happy,
While others made me sad.

But what am I to do with them?
Disregard them totally?
Or live and learn from what I've done,
Thus, improving life for me.

I'll hand on to good memories,
And learn from each mistake,
Thereby in the future,
A much better person I'll make.

To really understand oneself,
Is just no easy task,
That's why I have to daily look at,
Just "Who Am I".......and ask????

LATE

A behavior that is IRRITATING, is always being late,
To others it's disrespectful, it's their feelings you berate,
It's as if they're not acknowledged, being late is simply crude,
And because you're not on time, to other's you are rude.

When being late continues, there are feelings of disdain,
Then others limit contact...and with you don't entertain.
A behavior of **self-centeredness,** it really is unkind,
Soon no one will make plans with you, and you'll be left behind.

When we are healthy people, what we say and DO, we trust,
We keep our plans, show up on time, our word it is must.
So,...when making plans with others and you set a time and date,
If you **RESPECT YOURSELF** and **THEM**, you'll find you won't be

LATE!

LEARN HOW TO BE

I can feel I've accomplished a lot in a day,
   If I just take time to be **STILL** and to **PRAY.**
I don't have to run around in a "tiz,"
   Doing "this or that" like I'm some kind of "wiz'."
To **BE** and relax is what I need to do,
   It's the greatest gift I can give myself, too.
To trample myself always running around,
   Is really quite "sick"...there's no peace to be found.
If I sit and I pray and converse with my God,
   It's so unfamiliar, it sometimes seems odd.
So I have to practice and just take the time,
   To **LISTEN** to Him, so life gets sublime.
It's in those quiet moments, that **I HEAR HIS WORDS,**
   I gaze upon nature...see the trees and the birds.
What a wonderful world, God sent us to see,
   If I just take time....and **LEARN HOW TO "BE."**

LIFE IS WHAT I MAKE IT

I sit here thinking of life and love,
And my Higher Power up above,
We're born, we live, someday we die,
There's things we do, we don't know why,
We make mistakes and through the pain,
We grow and change and aren't the same.
For some of us, the struggle's hard,
We go through battles burned and scarred.
Our feelings sometimes are confused;
They're "up and down," our hearts are bruised.
But errors somehow make us grow,,
And we're **IMPATIENT** 'cause growth is slow.
And then one day we get in touch,
For God has given us so much.
We learn to talk and feel and share,
And for ourselves we learn to care.
We then take charge of things we do,
And use our **FAITH** to help us through,
For every day the sun can shine,
If I like **MYSELF**, the world is mine.

LORD HELP ME......

Lord help me to change to let go of "my way"
and help me to live and BE for today.
Help me to know who I am, how I feel;
I don't want to pretend, but be open and real.
Help me to overcome trial and pain,
and look for the good, changing losses to gain.
Help me to reach out and ask for my needs,
and through my mistakes, I'll know what to heed.
I can't change my past and tomorrow's not here;
If I work on today, I'll have nothing to fear.
I'll let go of the guilt, put behind all the sorrow
and not be concerned for the things of tomorrow.
I can't CONTROL others, or how they will be;
Please give me the strength just to take care of me.
I'll learn how to love and FEEL and be fine,
by walking with you "one day at a time!"

Dedicated to all those I have known, on this
"road to recovery."

MARY, MOTHER OF SORROWS

There was a young woman, so holy and pure,
   That when God said He'd send us His Son,
He thought she should be the mother of God,
   For her goodness, yes she was the one.
She was only 15 when given the news,
   The angel told her, she would give birth
To a male child, the son of God,
   As our Savior, He'd be sent to earth,
She said as the handmaiden of the Lord,
   She would do whatever God's will,
And so on that glorious Christmas morn,
   Jesus came, prophecy was fulfilled.
Yes, she was **His Mom,** and He was her child,
   She held Him, and **fed** Him.....**took care,**
Of all the things He did as a boy,
   As His mother, she always was there.
Right up to the end, when nailed on a cross,
   Oh, the pain and the suffering and grief
To see the young man, the son that she loved,
   Hanging there, right next to the thief.
The crowd that abused, made fun of her son,
   As she cried as a mother would do,
For this little boy whom she held in her arms
   Was being humiliated, too.
For this she is called the "Mother of Sorrows."
   And she showed us just how we should act,
Admit we are sad....**cry** in our pain,
   And **LET GO**...for to God He went back.

MOST AT PEACE

I'm most at PEACE, when there's no one around,
And the Dear Lord and I can hang out,
For it's in those conversations with **HIM**,
That I'm left, without any doubt.

That the **"spiritual"** life, is the journey I'm on,
Together we'll get through each day,
For He's my best friend, and loves me the most,
So, I listen to what He has to say.........LIKE

Unless we're converted and become as children,
Heaven's kingdom...we cannot enter,
It means that we're **"LITTLE"**, and in His hands,
Of our world and life, He's the center.

He gets disappointed, "Oh, ye of little faith,"
When we don't **SEEK** out His care,
He wants us to **ASK**, and **KNOCK** on His door,
For He said He would always be there!

So, we sit and talk, and then I just **LISTEN**,
And His words become very clear,
The message He wants to convey to me most
Is **FEAR NOT**, for I'm always near!

MATURITY.... HEALTHY COPING

An indication of maturation in life,
    is when we learn **DELAYED GRATIFICATION**,
and other healthy coping skills,
    like **improved communication**.
What is it **I feel and need?**
    How do I share that with another?
Without self-centeredness and pride,
    or blaming problems on others.
I learn I have the ability,
    to solve my problems each day,
I pick **"role models"** to emulate,
    for they can show me the way.
I no longer, minimize, justify,
    everything that I am doing,
I **make healthy choices** for my life,
    so the things that are ensuing.....
will bring me peace and happiness,
    not trauma, chaos and sorrow,
and **use the tools God gave** to me,
    and not be afraid about tomorrow.

I put myself in **situations** I know,
    are **good and beneficial** for me.
I **don't judge others** or what they do,
    that way, I'm emotionally free.
I inventory my strengths and weakness,
    and change what I am able,
so I feel peace, down deep within,
    and what "I bring to the table."
I **don't put up with abuse or attacks,**
    or allow that I be mistreated.
Stay calm, and cool and dignified,
    even when conversations get "heated."
For others are not my prime focus today,
    I've no need for drugs or booze,
for if I reach for them to cope,
    that's negative and I'll lose.
No longer with anger, fear or resentment,
    I love myself and others, too,
Forgive the past, what has been done.
    Each day... I begin ANEW!!!

THANK YOU GOD FOR EACH NEW BEGINNING!

OUT OF THE NEST

Our children aren't ours, to take care of for life,
  They come to us ...and through us, you see,
They are with us 'til adulthood they reach,
  Then out on their own, they need be.
For we are to **TEACH** them to **care for themselves,**
  Be **responsible,** and know how to live,
To be out on their own, without all our help,
  For themselves they must take care and give.
If we don't **let go, and dependent** they are,
  On us for their life off the street,
We've not done our job, helping them with the skills,
  Not knowing how to live and compete.
They just lean on us and we simply take over,
  The running and care of their lives,
There's more harm than good in things that we do.
  For it's on us they depend to survive.
How **selfish** is this, that we don't give to them,
  The **dignity** to struggle and try?
And learn from mistakes, the way we all did,
  If we don't, then we're helping them die.

We get in the way, of their growing up,
  We're telling them that they are unable,
For we're taking care of the things they should do,
  It's implying that **they are incapable.**
Just like the animals whose "babes" leave the nest,
  As soon as they're able to fly,
We must do the same with these children of ours,
  Or they'll never know how to **SURVIVE.**
In order that each of them learn **self worth,**
  We must teach them to be **self-sufficient,**
And they can't do that, if we're running their life,
  And of nothing are they ever proficient.
So we **LOVE** them enough, to **LET GO** and **LET GOD,**
  To guide them on their path and journey,
And smile as they go, knowing full well,
  They can make it, for life's about **LEARNING!!!**

MY INVENTORY

As the days in the year are winding down,
And the bells ring in the NEW,
I need to **INVENTORY** my life,
And see just how I DO?

What is it I like about myself?
What behaviors do I want to keep?
Which parts are useful to my God?
Are there things I need to seek?

Is my attitude real positive?
Do my deeds help me and mankind?
What side of me is negative, and
What new ways do. I need to find?

I'll set some **GOALS** for this new year,
For my life, I need a vision,
It's imperative I make some change,
Or remain in "my own prison."

My **PERCEPTION**, it impairs my life,
When not a healthy view,
God please give me the **WILLINGNESS**,
To change things I think and do.

I need to be **AWARE** this year,
Of the things that cause me **PAIN**.
The problem lies within my head,
When my thinking isn't sane.

A "victim" I no longer am,
I've taken control of **MY** life,
If I allow others to dictate to me,
It results in hurt and strife.

A healthy person is **POSITIVE**,
Has **FAITH** in the power on high.
It's hard enough to take care of me,
To fix others....I won't even try!

I'll concentrate on God's will for me,
And focus on my well-being,
Stay out of **DENIAL** and not **MINIMIZE**,
So **REALITY**, I will be seeing.

I'll **ASK** for my needs and **SAY** what I feel,
I'll I **MIND MY OWN BUSINESS**, that's key,
If I can do this for myself all year,
My life will be simple and free.

OUTCOMES...in GOD'S HANDS

I'm responsible for myself,
   And take care the best that I can.
I'm the only one I have control of,
   And all **OUTCOMES**, they're in **GOD'S HANDS!**
I make up my mind, to do this or that,
   And think it's a positive decision,
But if not in my interest, God will make sure,
   And there will be a **revision**.
Things don't always go the way that I want,
   So, I just do my best day by day,
I'm confident I have my God in my life,
   And I trust He will show me the way!

THE POSTCARD

As I gaze at the fall colors,
of red and green and orange and brown,
My Higher Power sent a **POSTCARD**,
telling me that He's around.

With each and every color,
I know that He is near,
And as the leaves fall to the ground,
He tells me "have no fear."

Soon these trees will be dormant,
and they'll take a winter's rest,
And in the spring they'll grow again
and will survive another test.

I am forever grateful
that He shares this scene with me,
'cause the beauty of all nature is:
"It's absolutely free."

It's as if my Higher Power said,
"I'm our here in plain sight;
I've always been here by your side,
whether you were wrong or right."

And as I marvel at those shades,
and the sun and sky above.
I know He sent this **POSTCARD**,
with His undying **LOVE**.

THE POWER OF PRAYER

It seems that my recent revelation is this:
    That I need to **LISTEN** and **LEARN**.
A "spiritual" journey is what I am on,
    My soul is my greatest concern.
For I have to trust...to travel with God,
    Who leads me each step of the way.
My spirit within needs His guidance and love,
    And through **PRAYER**, I receive it all day.
When I try to control, and do things on my own,
    I forget that the power's in WE,
My God, the BOOK, my friends, the 12-Steps,
    With them, I can learn and can see.
Just how I'm supposed to be leading MY LIFE,
    Leaving others to lives of their own.
Not trying to **CONTROL** what others will do,
    A behavior, to which I am prone.
The answers I've found, while conversing with God,
    The **SOLUTIONS** that **PRAYER** brings to mind
The love and forgiveness of others and self,
    Is through God, no where else could I find.
I've learned not to stay in the **PROBLEM** too long,
    CHANGE MY THINKING to what's good for me,
I surrender myself to His guidance through PRAYER,
    To be JOYOUS,.. HOPEFUL...AND FREE.

"PRAY WITHOUT CEASING"

"PRAY WITHOUT CEASING " THE Bible tells us,
   Constantly converse with the THREE,
      The FATHER, the SON, HOLY SPIRIT OF GOD,
For they protect and help us to see.

When we are adrift, on the sea we call life,
   With no **POWER** or rudder that's strong,
      They keep us away from **TEMPTATIONS** and fears,
      And a path, if we go down, is wrong!

We have to stay in touch with our GOD,
   Who will give us the strength how to act,
      For **PRAYER** gives the power, to do the right things,
      Instead of sinking, our life is intact.

Even tho' busy.... we can talk anytime,
   And GOD listens to us....our concerns,
      Then we need be quiet, for the answers HE sends,
      There's HIS message we get in return.

So we can daily **"PRAY WITHOUT CEASING,"**
   It's the time that we find most well spent.
      Enjoying our conversations with God,
      For HIS LOVE for us never relents.

PRIDE

My Mom said, "**PRIDE** goeth .....BEFORE a fall!"
A DETRIMENTAL behavior, it's true,
It impacts my life in a negative way,
For it says I am better than you!

PRIDE is one of the deadliest sins,
It raises me up above others,
That's not the way Christ intended I be,
He said we're all "sisters and brothers."

For I am no better, than anyone else,
When it comes to the love of the Savior,
So I set **PRIDE** aside.... have intentions be pure,
With **SELF-HONESTY** my chief motivator.

PRO FOOTBALL.....FAME AND GLORY

(Dedicated to B.B. ....ALL PRO.....DB)

There's nothing more exhilarating, than a hit that I dish out,
  As a lean and mean defensive back, you punish, bang and shout.
The adrenalin gets flowing, it's like being in a war,
  And every time you take one out, say, "com'on just give me more!"
More to throw my body at...and more to hit real hard
  More to cover and defend, it's like an "animal yard."
I rush, I stunt, I pass defend...let out a grueling yell,
  And in the trenches, when at war, it really feels like h--l!
I dearly love those battle days, with shirt down to my knees,
  The blood and bruises, bumps and scars, cold weather when I
    freeze!
The crowds, the cheers, the accolades, feel great when we're
    on top,
  The "boo's", the jeers, the bad mouthing...have to silence,
    have to stop.
I cannot get discouraged on those days we find we lose,
  There ain't no time to sit around and cry and sing the blues.
I just get up, go out again, and do my job, at best,
  To make big plays, and help my team, and survive another test.
It's just another afternoon...a workday...wet or dry,
  I love it all, the ups and downs... sometimes I wonder why?
Those guys in stripes, they cramp my style...with flags that hit
    the ground,
"Can't help it ref, he dropped the ball...and then, he just **FELL
DOWN!"**
This game is such a part of me...the fame, prestige and glory,
  Yet, there's another side to me....but that's **ANOTHER
STORY!**

73

THE 12 STEP PROGRAM

IN .....

STEP I   we admitted our **POWERLESSNESS**
STEP 2   we came to believe,
               there is a **Higher Power** around,
               from whom we can find relief.
STEP 3   we made a decision,
               turn to God, give Him our will.
STEP 4   we took an **inventory,**
               for this, we need to be still.
STEP 5   we began admitting,
               the exact nature of our wrongs,
STEP 6   we're ready, to remove our **defects,**
               for this will make us strong.
STEP 7   we humbly asked Him,
               to remove our character flaws,
STEP 8   we made a list of people we'd harmed,
STEP 9   made amends to them all.
STEP 10   we continued an inventory,
               and promptly admitted mistakes,
STEP 11   through **meditation** and **prayer,**
               do **HIS WILL** with the power it takes.
STEP 12   we're to carry the **message,**
               to others, so they can, too, find ,
               the freedom from bondage that's given to us,
               when we **CHANGE** and we leave **PAST** behind.

This program's a **NEW WAY** of living,
Trust God, clean house,.....for it's known,
That's why the steps, all begin with **WE,**
'cause we can't make these changes **ALONE!**

PURE LOVE

God listens and He answers us,
With **YES**...or **NO**....or **WAIT**.
He always does what's best for us,
His timing's never late.
Sometimes we feel He's let us down
When we don't get our way,
That is the WILLFUL side of us,
And why we need to PRAY.
Yes, I know God has the PLAN,
For my life...that's way above,
Anything that I desire,
Because He is **PURE LOVE**.

REMEMBER THE PAIN

Lord, thank you for the happiness,
But I'll not forget the pain,
Because if I remember it,
I won't make the mistakes AGAIN!

I DON'T KNOW

I don't know where I'm going,
But I sure know where I've been,
And a new way has got to be better,
So, I'm not going that way again!!!

END....BEGINNING

Sometimes there has to be an end,
For there to be a beginning,
What often appears to be a loss,
Can actually be a winning.

THE REQUIREMENTS

What does the Lord **REQUIRE** of me?
Of me... just what does **HE ASK?**

Be **FAIR** and **JUST** and **MERCIFUL,**
HUMBLY WALK with **GOD** .... just simple tasks!
   (Micah 6:8)

Then what are the gifts He gives in return?
What does He want.... **FOR ME?**

Do the things He asks, follow **HIS WORD,**
So I'm **HAPPY, JOYOUS** and **FREE.**
   (AA Big Book 133)

THE RIVER FLOWS

I live on the land where the river runs by,
Where the birds, ducks and geese, overhead...do fly.
The woods come up...to my deck....I can see,
As the deer, raccoons, bunnies and chipmunks run free.

I give food to the critters...the birds sunflower seeds,
Delight watching the animals and all the birds feed.
I find peace, joy, contentment, daily living this scene.
With my Father in heaven...I am soooo serene.

Yes, the river flows freely ... birds and animals abound,
It's where GOD'S WORLD'S apparent....and HIS LOVE is found.

SAUL TO PAUL

Many people just do THEIR WILL,
As did a man named Saul,
Then God, He knocked him off his horse,
And his name was changed to PAUL.

Through this event he saw the "light"
'bout his cunning, baffling ways.
He turned his life over to his God.
And forever gave Him praise.

He traveled 'round, to spread the word,
"good news" about his Savior,
The one who gave him strength inside,
To forgive and change behaviors.

Sometimes the hardest things in life,
Events that seem the worst,
Are the best....but at the time,
We feel that we'll just burst.

But God, He knows, and has the PLAN,
Like when Paul fell to the ground,
It's only through events like that,
That we change our life around.

SLOGANS

There's many great slogans to help us,
  For instance, there's **LISTEN** and **LEARN,**
We have to stay tuned for God's messages,
  For answers in life to discern,
There's **FIRST THINGS FIRST** and **EASY DOES IT,**
  And **ONE DAY AT A TIME,**
These will help us, stay centered inside,
  So peace and contentment we find.
Also.....**HOW IMPORTANT IS IT?**
  That makes us stop and **THINK.**
To sort out our reactions,
  So they're healthy and not sick,
For we learn to **KEEP IT SIMPLE,**
  And **KEEP AN OPEN MIND,**
So we're not locked into old messages,
  That, to us, were not very kind.
To **LET GO and LET GOD,** and live **JUST FOR TODAY,**
  We must **LET IT BEGIN WITH ME,**
If we follow the steps, go to meetings and read,
  Live the slogans, we learn how to **BE!**

SOMETIMES LIFE UNRAVELS

Sometimes life's like a ball of yarn,
It just starts to unravel,
What seems to be the cause of this,
Is the road I CHOOSE to travel.

If I make HEALTHY choices,
My life just hums along
Like the lilting melody,
In the sweetness of a song.

However, if I force my will,
Not consult with God instead.
My world it crashes down on me,
'Cause my "SPIRIT" life is dead.

God tells me to "let go" and place,
All others in HIS hands,
Do the healthy things for me,
Because HE has the PLAN.

I must remember that my God,
Wants nothing more for me,
Than to follow HIS DIRECTIONS,
So that I can live happily.

THE SPIRITUAL JOURNEY

I'm on a **SPIRITUAL JOURNEY,,**
  To get closer to my God,
I need more revelations,
  As along this path I trod.
I need **LISTEN** to HIS message,
  And understand HIS word,
Read about those friends of His,
  And learn what they have heard,
Like St. Therese and St. Francis,
  Who were examples of His way,
For they were very simple,
  Be as children's, what they'd say.
The relationship of God and I,
  Is like a child and Dad,
He loves me oh, so very much,
  HE comforts when I'm sad,
But He said....I need to know,
  I am to "HAVE NO FEAR,"
Because whatever comes along,
  He'll protect me that is clear.
I have to live that **"child like"** faith,
  And trust my God above,
And ask for graces for His will,
  Knowing it is me HE LOVES.

STAY IN TODAY

I must learn to **FOCUS**...to **STAY IN TODAY**,
   Or else my thoughts, they just wander,
They bounce all over, go here and there,
   The ideas, I ponder and conjure.

Like things I need do....and places to go,
   This all in my **mind** does transpire,
I drive down the road...**thinking** these things,
   Next thing, I'm exhausted and tired.

And none of this has even happened, as yet,
   It's simply my **thoughts** going wild,
I need calm down, and stay in the now,
   With the simplicity of a little child,

For if I don't, I will miss all the gifts,
   The blessings my God sends each day,
So I will slow down, change my **thinking** around,
   And not let my **thoughts** go astray.

STUDENT.....TEACHER

When the student is ready,
  The teacher will appear,
    This is not necessarily true,
      Sometimes it's the teacher,
        Who learns from the student,
So, who is to say who....is who?

RISE UP

Engage in conversations
  With the Dear Lord all day long,
Don't entertain any negative thoughts....
  That's not where we belong.
Expect the Lord will hear our plea,
  When we ask for what we need,
Then **RISE UP** to receive HIS GIFTS
  We need them to succeed.

SUFFER IN SILENCE

When is it our first suffering begins?
   It starts with the secrets we keep.
In silence we bury the feelings we have,
   And get either angry or weep,
With one and then two... and soon there are more.
   We stockpile them up all inside,
We learn to keep quiet, not say a thing,
   And soon all our feelings we hide.
But the only person getting sick is ourselves,
   As others go on with their lives,
And one day we realize that we're hurting us,
   And it's not just enough to survive.
We need to be open, honest and willing,
   To admit that our feelings have meaning,
Find people to share with...be truthful with them,
   In so doing, an inside housecleaning.
We need to admit the feelings we have,
   Speak out 'bout the things that transpired,
We don't need "act out" or stuff anymore,
   From this behavior, we really have tired.
To say what we feel, and ask for our needs,
   To no longer feel angry, keep score
Life has new meaning and we're free to be,
   And in SILENCE SUFFER no more!

SUNLIGHT OF THE SPIRIT

In the "sunlight of the spirit,"
Is the place we want to stroll,
　Gently going through our days,
　A pace good for the soul,
For God made us His children,
For His pleasure, bring Him joy,
　It was for His glory that,
　He made us, girl and boy.
Yet, we forget who He is,
And idly run around,
　Busy rushing through our lives
　With EGO'S we abound.
But EGO'S only Ease...God...Out,
Instead of going to Him,
　There is no glory for our God,
　Our lives become a ruin,
In the "sunlight of the spirit,"
Is where direction's found,
　Conversing with our Lord of love,
　And in His joy abound.

He likes when He can help us,
We beseech His holy name,
  And whether anxious, happy, sad,
  He's there for us the same.
For when we bring our problems,
Fears and sorrows,... everything,
  He smiles at us and takes them all,
  Because He is our king,
His joy is reaching out to us,
He loves when we are caring,
  We laugh and cry and seek His help,
  With Him, our lives we're sharing.
The way's not always known to us,
That's why we ask the spirit,
  For directions in our life,
  Then LISTEN, so we hear it.
His "spirit's sunshine" lights our way,
Our best and truest guide,
  For He wants US ... to be HIS FRIEND,
  With Him, walk side by side.

SURRENDER

To **SURRENDER** my will to the will of God,
   Is the **ESSENCE** of the **SPIRITUAL** way.
For I rest as a child in the Father's arms,
   Trusting He will protect me each day.
The thing to **FEAR** is to take **MY WILL** back,
   And just do what I want to do.
So, I pray for the knowledge of **HIS WILL** for me,
   And the **POWER** to carry it through.

TWELVE

The number **12** has significant meaning,
   There are **12** (times two) hours in a day,
And Jesus, He chose **12** apostles as friends,
   And it's with them, that He asked to pray.
And also we find, **12** months in a year,
   And THE **12** DAYS OF CHRISTMAS, we sing.
But in recovery....the most **IMPORTANT** of all,
   The **12 STEPS** and the **SERENITY** they bring.

THANKSGIVING

On the eve of this Thanksgiving,
   with a **HUMBLE ATTITUDE**,
For all the gifts God's given me,
   I have such **GRATITUDE**.
He's given me a **FAITH** that's strong,
   To know He's always near,
And any problem that I face,
   With Him, to have **"NO FEAR."**
I'm grateful for my health, family,
   And friends who are around,
And for my home and food to eat,
   The **SERENITY** I've found.
The choir in which I'm blessed to sing,
   As we raise up one voice,
To sing the praises of our God,
   In whom, we can rejoice.
My children are a precious gift,
   Grandchildren are a plus,
Even with the "ups and downs,"
   When they seem to make a fuss.
There's not enough that I can say,
   'bout the goodness of my God,
Give **THANKS** to Him this special day,
   For the journey that I trod.

THE FLOCK

There are **FOUR MUSTS** to our recovery,
   If we are to be clean and serene,
We read the **books,** get a **sponsor** and **meet,**
   Do the **steps**... for they are supreme.!
They bring us serenity day after day,
   And teach us a new way to live,
So we never let go of these wonderful tools,
   For we stay and help others we give!
If we ever get lazy and let any go,
   We'll soon find our misery is back,
Our thinking, addictions are active again,
   'cause we've completely fallen off track.
So, again we attend our good meetings with friends,
   And find that no matter the weather,
If we want to continue with clean and serene,
   It's us **BIRDS,** we must all **FLOCK** together.

ANOTHER SLOGAN

Sponsors don't hesitate to say this,
   Go to meetings!......Yes, we are!
    So we need to add a new slogan,
     And it is just...."**GET IN THE CAR!**"

THE MEEK SHALL INHERIT ....

When Jesus said "the meek shall inherit the earth."
He wasn't talking of our world that's surrounded,
He meant how I **THINK**, will dictate my actions,
So, inner thoughts, with **HIM**, must be grounded.

It's not all the things that happen in life,
Whether stressful, sad or exciting,
It's how I **CHOOSE** to react to them all,
So, my thoughts I need to be righting.

For there's many things that simply occur,
Over which I have no control,
Christ called the "meek", those tuned into God,
Who strive to save their own soul.

The "meek" are those who are mentally sound,
And look to God for the way,
They know they can't go on by themselves,
They listen to what He has to say.

For if my thinking is aligned with God's
It doesn't matter what happens each day,
All that transpires, I'll know what to do.
I'll **ACCEPT**, makes **CHANGES** and **PRAY**.

The things of earth will never dictate,
The kind of person to be,
That comes from INSIDE, as the Dear Lord said,
For with HIM, I am always free.
                for "the meek shall inherit the earth"
                        (**Meek as Moses)**

THERESE, THE LITTLE FLOWER

There was once a girl named Therese..
  Of The Child Jesus and The Holy Face,
    God sent her to earth, so that she could teach us,
      It is HIM that we need to embrace.
At age fifteen, she entered the convent,
  Mom died.. she was in Papa's care,
    She asked the Pope for permission for this,
      For her sisters were already there.
She taught us about what's called her LITTLE WAY,
  For she was the simplest of souls,
    Just offer to God all the **MENIAL** tasks,
      For that's all we really control.
Her soul abounded with love and joy,
  To see Mary and His Holy Face,
    The only fear she ever expressed,
      Was the transition from here to that place.
She knew the Lord cares, watches over us all,
  Just like lilies out in the field,
    And so to find peace and serenity
      To **HIS WILL** we must learn how to yield.
She was kind to all even those who brought gloom,
  She would smile.. and show some restraint,
    Not blurting out her negative thoughts,
      That's how she became such a **SAINT**.
She studied God's word and the Lord was her **FRIEND**,
  Never leaving the convent confines,
    And the statue of Mary that smiled down of her,
      Got her through all her **SUFFERING** times.

Patroness of the Missions and Doctor of Church,
  Is how we would all come to know her,
    And this **LITTLE FLOWER**, endearingly called,
      Said from heaven she send us a shower.
She's known for her roses, and the words that she spoke,
  Her life was of **S-I-M-P-L-I-C-I-T-Y**.
    She was an EXAMPLE of her **LITTLE WAY**,
      It's the only way to be free.
She knew of her frailties and human weakness,
  And asked that God help her... please **HIM**,
    For this little girl, full of wisdom and grace,
      did everything to avoid sin.
We must find inside that **CHILD LIKE FAITH**,
  Which the Father expects us to have,
    She mastered this task in her young and brief life,
      God was simply her **HEAVENLY DAD**.
She loved all God's nature, the birds and the flowers,
  And the beauty of all He created,
    And in her book...*THE STORY OF A SOUL*
      The truths of her life....she related.
What a wonderful model of how to live life,
  One day at a time we'll be shown,
    That knowing no matter what troubles we face,
      With our God, we are **NEVER ALONE**.
Yes, this **LITTLE FLOWER**, who struggled in life,
  And offered her Dear Lord her **PAIN**,
    Looked for the day, when united with **HIM**,
      She would there, forever, remain.
She was just twenty-four, with her mission completed,
  When she looked upon His **HOLY FACE**,
    Her gift to us ... was share her LITTLE WAY,
      And see **ROSES**....and back to her trace.

THE STORY OF LOVE

It was on this glorious Christmas morn,
    That....the Son of God was born,
He lay in a manger, a bed of straw,
    Joseph, Mary and angels, smiled in awe,
The animals were on bended knee,
    Three wise men came, their king to see,
From there to carpenter shop, to preacher,
    He became our healer and our teacher,
From babe in a manger, so lowly and frail,
    He bore our sins, on a cross, hung with nails,
He loved us all and for us He died,
    As mother and brother, looked on and cried,
His mission in life was over and done,
    He was our Savior, and truly God's son,
For at that moment, heaven's gate opened wide,
    Our sins were forgiven, we could enter inside,
'twas this Christmas morning, so long, long ago,
    That God sent His son, so **HIS LOVE** we would know.

THE TRIP

I enter the world, alone with God,
  And leave it the same lovely way,
I better be good, to the one on the trip,
  If not, it is I who will pay!

When I put others....ahead of me,
  And not get my needs met at all,
That is what's called **CODPENDENCY**,
  And that behavior will cause me to fall.

I still need to be compassionate,
  And for others, have care and concern,
However, I have to be good to myself,
  To love me....have faith....live and learn.

God said, "love thy neighbor as **thyself**,"
  That means I must take care of me,
Then reach out in service, to others with love,
  For it's our God, in others, we see.

THREE PERSONS IN ONE

The FATHER created the sky, sun and stars,
 The moon, trees and flowers...for His glory,
He added the oceans, animals and man,
 And in Genesis, we find the whole story.
The **SON** came to earth, in a stable was born,
 To redeem us was why He was sent,
 For 33 years, performed miracles and preached,
 And simply asked all to repent.
He died on a cross made of wood, on a hill,
 In the saddest and cruelest of ways,
 Yet, he bore our sins, as the prophets foretold,
 In the Bible, it tells of those days.
HOLY SPIRIT of God, who inspires us all,
 Gives us **guidance, knowledge** and **truth,**
 Divine wisdom is always flowing through us,
 If we're **open,** this inspiration's profuse.
As we grow and we change on this journey we're on,
 We look for good orderly direction,
 And we learn to live, one day at a time,
 For the future, we have no projections.

The **HOLY SPIRIT,** third person, who guides us all,
  When our hearts and minds are open,
    Through **quiet reflection, contemplation** and **prayer,**
    Inspiration to us is spoken.
It's not the material things in life,
  That make us happy or whole,
    It's only by God flowing through us in truth,
    That new knowledge is revealed to our soul.
For we need **HIS** guidance and miraculous help,
  For protection, each step of the way,
    And when our journey in life is complete,
    Entering heaven, we'll hear our God say,
"Welcome my dear and faithful servant,
  You've known **FATHER, HOLY SPIRIT** and **SON,**
    You've listened well, and walked the walk,
    Welcome home....your job is done."

TRUTH......HONESTY

TRUTH...is about the WORDS that I speak,
   I say them without a "forked-tongue,"
It's with TRUTHFULNESS that I utter my speech,
   And others trust where I'm coming from.

HONESTY...is an inner value of mine,
   It's means I have no self-deception,
Often, when I'm in DENIAL of things,
   My mind has a faulty "perception,"
So I can be truthful...a lie never tell,
   With myself be dishonest...deceived,
A behavior of which I want to be rid,
   With SELF-HONESTY, my life is retrieved.

So I TELL the TRUTH.....am HONEST with SELF,
   With this will come joy.....satisfaction,
Because my words and insides agree,
   And I won't have to make a retraction.

TURN THEM OVER

Everyone's always in **GOD'S HANDS**,
   It's my duty to leave them all there,
They only become my burden in life,
   When their problems become MY affair.
Why do I take them out of **GOD'S HANDS**,
   And place them upon my own plate?
So, I can dictate what I think's best for them,
   I'm their "keeper" in charge of their fate?
Direct what they say and then what they do,
   Be in charge of their comings and goings,
I don't even give them the dignity to run...
   Their own lives....now that's really "mind-blowing."
For they have a God who's in charge of their world,
   And HE does better work than I do,
So, I **TURN THEM OVER**, back into **GOD'S HANDS**,
   And make sure that I jump in there, too!!!

TURN THE OTHER CHEEK...

When Christ said to us..."**to turn other cheek..**"
   He didn't mean let someone hit you,
He meant **TURN AWAY** from our **THINKING** instead,
   So, of problems, we get a new **VIEW**.
It's our **THINKING** that gets us in trouble in life,
   And if someone treats us mean and cruel,
We don't have to be...subjected to that,
   "turn our cheek," change our **THINKING**, new rule,
Not to allow ourselves be mistreated,
   To **THINK** we're **God's child**, have **SELF-WORTH**,
Our **THINKING** the source of the problems we have,
   So we change to have **PEACE** upon earth.
Yes, we **"turn our cheek,"** so we **TURN AWAY**,
   What others may do is their problem,
Our **THINKING** gets better when we **TURN TO GOD**,
   And with **HIM**, our own problems, **WE'll SOLVE THEM.**

UNCONDITIONAL LOVE

What is the boundary between **UNCONDITIONAL LOVE,**
   and tolerating **INAPPROPRIATE BEHAVIOR?**
      To answer this question, we simply need,
         to look at the words from Our Savior,
He said "Love your neighbor AS YOURSELF,"
   so, if I care and respect **HE made ME,**
      I love all others as children of God,
         NOT INAPPROPRIATE BEHAVIOR, you see!
Because all it does is tear me down,
   belittle me, then I feel bad,
      I need not defend myself anymore,
         or allow mistreatment where I feel sad.
I am to cherish, the gift of **MYSELF**
   and not be attacked or abused.
      For if I allow **INAPPROPRIATE BEHAVIOR,**
         I'll feel angry, "victimized"...used.
I must love and value who I am,
   and make sure to my 'OWN SELF BE TRUE,
      I pray for all **others**, with **UNCONDITIONAL LOVE,**
         knowing God will take care of them, TOO!

WE GAIN STRENGTH

Life is composed of experiences,
Some both good and bad,
When we fall and hurt ourselves,
We shouldn't stay down and sad.

Life is an "uphill" battle,
There's no way to "breeze" through,
Just how well we handle it,
Is up to me and you.

There are some things that we do,
For a while seem negative,
Never think of them as that,
They **TEACH** us how to live.

Like in youth, the little boy,
Who fell and scraped his knee,
We learn from every time we fall,
It teaches us to heed.

'Cause every time we fall and hurt,
The **STRUGGLE** to our feet,
Overcoming these afflictions,
Makes us **STRONG** - not weak!

We must to **optimistic,**
Each event a stepping stone,
The Lord will help us through it,
So we **never** are **alone.**

    For He knows we're not perfect,
    And mistakes we're bound to make,
    What we need is fortitude,
    He gives us strength to take.

So never feel I guility,
About experiences you've had,
They all turn into POSITIVES,
We improve and should be glad.

    For those who never err and fall,
    Simply remain the same,
    It's only those who take a CHANCE.
    Who have EVERYTHING TO GAIN!

WHAT I'M DOING

I JUST HAVE TO KNOW WHAT I'M DOING!

That's what's most **IMPORTANT** to me,
For if I don't, I'm just set adrift,
On a sea of all others' mercy.

They'll dictate my comings and goings,
And everything that I do,
I won't even have a life of my own,
I've belittled myself just for you.

I find that I'm angry.... resentful,
And blame others for all of my strife,
And yet nobody makes me do this,
I willingly give up **MY LIFE**.

So I take back the power of **CHOICES**
And DECIDE the things I need to do,
Then how others fit in, will simply take place,
For I've kept.....**TO THINE OWN SELF BE TRUE!**

WHAT'S IN STORE

Of the future, I've no knowledge....and I'm surely glad of that,
 Because if I knew of it.... I'd **DIRECT** it, that's a fact!
I'd simply get in my way, having done it times before,
 Until I learned my lesson, knock and leave it at HIS door,
I simply know what I do, focus one day at a time,
 Why others do ... or act that way? There's no reason or no rhyme.
It's really not my business, to figure their lives out,
 When I start to do this, its my thoughts I need **REROUTE,**
Back to what I'm doing...am I being true to me?
 Saying what I feel and think and asking for my needs.
What the future holds for me, that's simply in God's power,
 He will make it known to me, by minute and by hour.
So, **LIFE** it's just unfolding, like the petal of the rose,
 Only He can do that, for it's only **HE** who knows!

WHERE I AM

I have what I need and that's all I want,
   I'm content WHERE I AM just to be,
      The Dear Lord takes care of me every day,
      And I'm grateful to HIM, yes indeed!

12 STEP MEETINGS

We need to go.....so that we can give,
   For that's how we help.....each other to live.

THOUGHTS

Our actions are always born in THOUGHTS
   And so we must keep them on track,
For if we don't, and the thinking gets sick,
   We can have all our misery back!

WINTER WONDERLAND

God painted a **"winter wonderland,"**
  With His white...snow-covered brush,
    Sometimes He needs to slow us down,
      As we're always in a rush.

With snow and ice, we take our time,
  And can **VIEW** His awesome glory,
    This winter scene, done with His hand,
      Reminds of the Christmas story,

I need to keep Him in my heart,
  All year, not just December,
    Reminded by this winter scene,
      Snow painted beauty, **His love**, I'll remember.

WITH YOU

I realize my GOAL in life,
   I must work my way to you,
I need to just remember this,
   In all I say and do,
Be kind to others and true to self,
   When wrong...apologize,
And use the talents you gave me,
   with your power, I realize.
For, if I put you first in life,
   The rest just comes with ease,
I mustn't worry, or have fear,
   It's you I need to please.
Since you're the king, and I'm you're kid,
   I'm sure you want the best,
For me, through my entire life,
   And at the end, **WITH YOU**, I'll rest.

WORRY....A NEGATIVE

Worry is a negative...for one's perceptions are unreal,
  It's one who carries cotton and believes he's toting steel,
He's accustomed to the world's weight to have upon his shoulder,
  And even when he's young in age, it makes him so much older.
For walking 'round with burden's piled, this strain can often tire,
  It even brings such pain and stress, one can easily expire.
Yes, worry is a package that we all need to divest,
  Just give to God, do what we can, and find in Him our rest.

HOW IMPORTANT IS IT?

How important is it? I have to ask myself each day,
  The little irritants in life, can lead my thoughts astray,
For if I let them wander, the problems, they will loom,
  And all the thoughts I'm having, will be of doom and gloom,
So I ask, **IS THIS IMPORTANT?** And the answer is a "NO!"
  Then all the anger and concern, will somehow fade and go.
For I have a God who's loving and has taken care of me.
  I'LL DO **MY PART**, and trust **HIS PLAN**, and it will be what it will be!

YOU ARE THE LIGHT

Sometimes, Dear Lord, this life of mine,
   Is more than I can handle,
At times like this, I pray to you,
   LIGHT my way, just like a candle.
Your "candlelight" shows me today,
   That I am not alone,
That you're my **LIGHT** and strength to bear,
   And my path, it will be shone.
For you're the **LIGHT** that guides us all,
   You've absolved all my misdeeds.
If you can do all that for me,
   What more is it I need?
I'll give to you, all that I have,
   My problems, fears and sorrows,
And once I do let go of them,
   I need not dread tomorrow,
My life becomes a life of joy,
   When you are my protector,
I give to you, my life to **LIGHT**,
   Because you are the DIRECTOR.

YOU CAN'T.......

You can't love someone who won't let you do it,
   and constantly pushes you away,
You can't give to one who doesn't accept,
   and must have everything their own way.
You can't control others...what they say or do,
   that's up to them .... for it is their choice,
You can't communicate with those deaf to us,
   and, with them,....we have no voice.
You can't get respect, from the selfish...self-centered,
   for of themselves...is all that they think,
You can't have **RELATIONSHIPS** with those who are stoned,
   for they have their drug and their drink,
You can't keep on giving to those who just take,
   for soon... all you have will be gone,
You can't operate out of guilt, fear, rejection,
   for the choices you make will be wrong.
We just have to care, and be good to ourselves,
   Then the choices we make will be true,
The best we can give, to **OURSELVES** on this day,
   And the others...... they'll find their way through.

IMPOSSIBLE

If at first you don't succeed, try,
   try again,
To attain things that are possible,
   NOT CHANGING her or him.
For it is **IMPOSSIBLE**,
   to have power to change another,
If that is what we're trying to do,
   we needn't even bother.
For we're just wasting our time,
   so what really is a MUST,
If we want to make some changes,
   then the one we **CHANGE IS US!!**